Coffee Lovers:
Adult Coloring Book

This book uses shapes provided by

www.Shapes4Free.com

Thanks Shapes4Free!

ISBN-13: 978-1530275830

ISBN-10: 1530275830

Imprint by Create Space

Printed in the United States of America

*Dedicated to everyone who always adds
another cup of coffee for a friend...*

COFFEE LOVERS

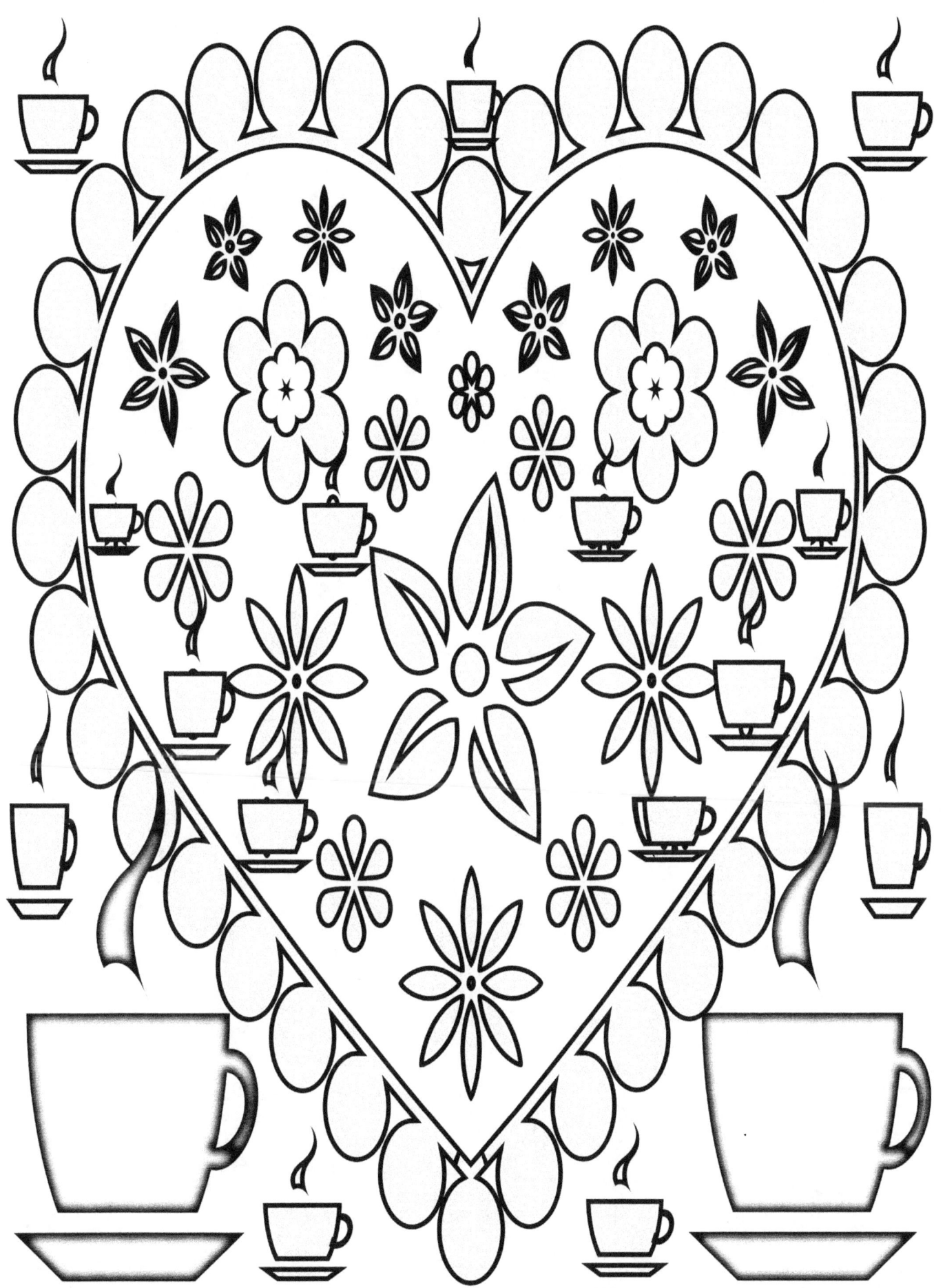

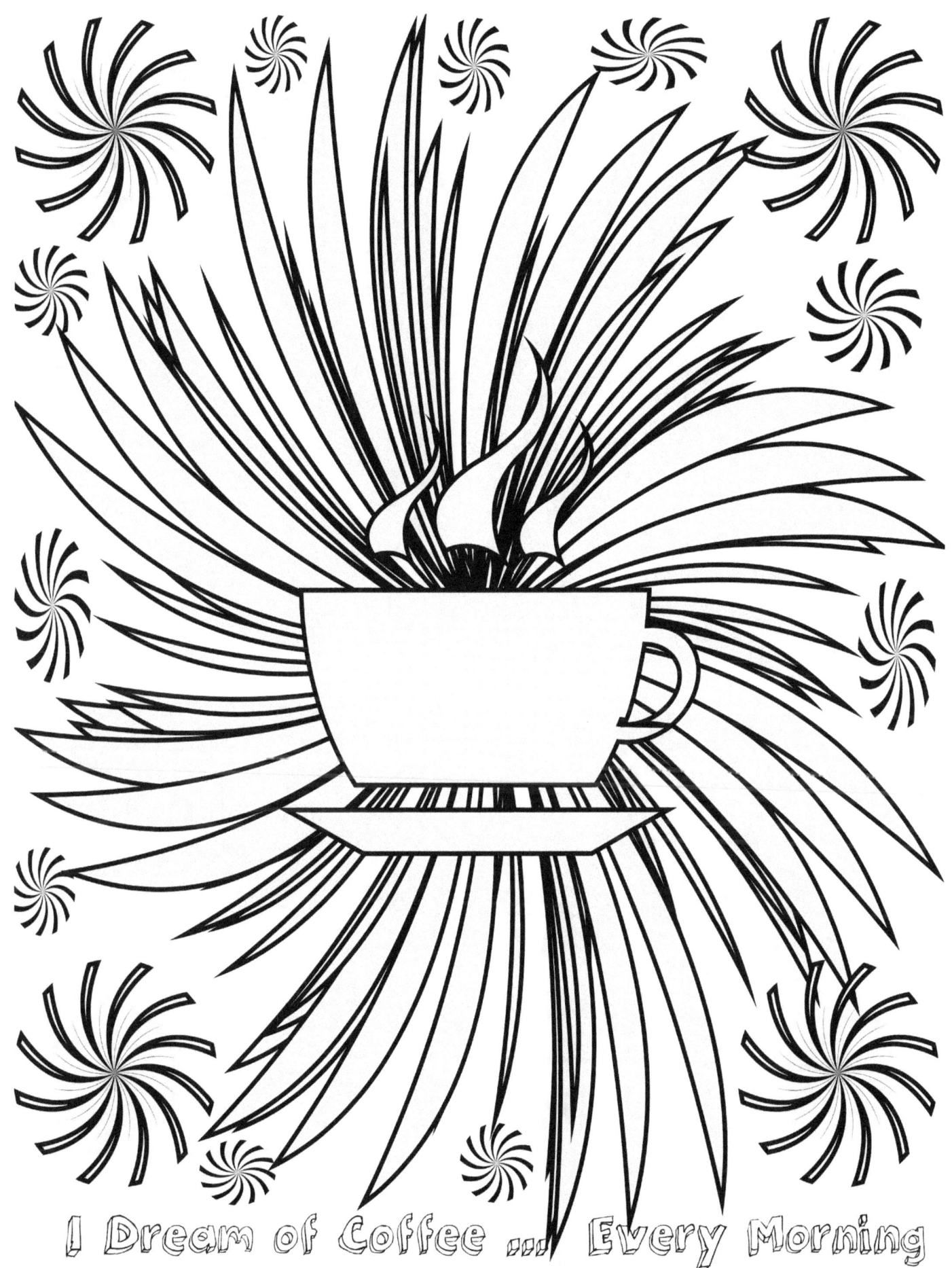

I Dream of Coffee ... Every Morning

13

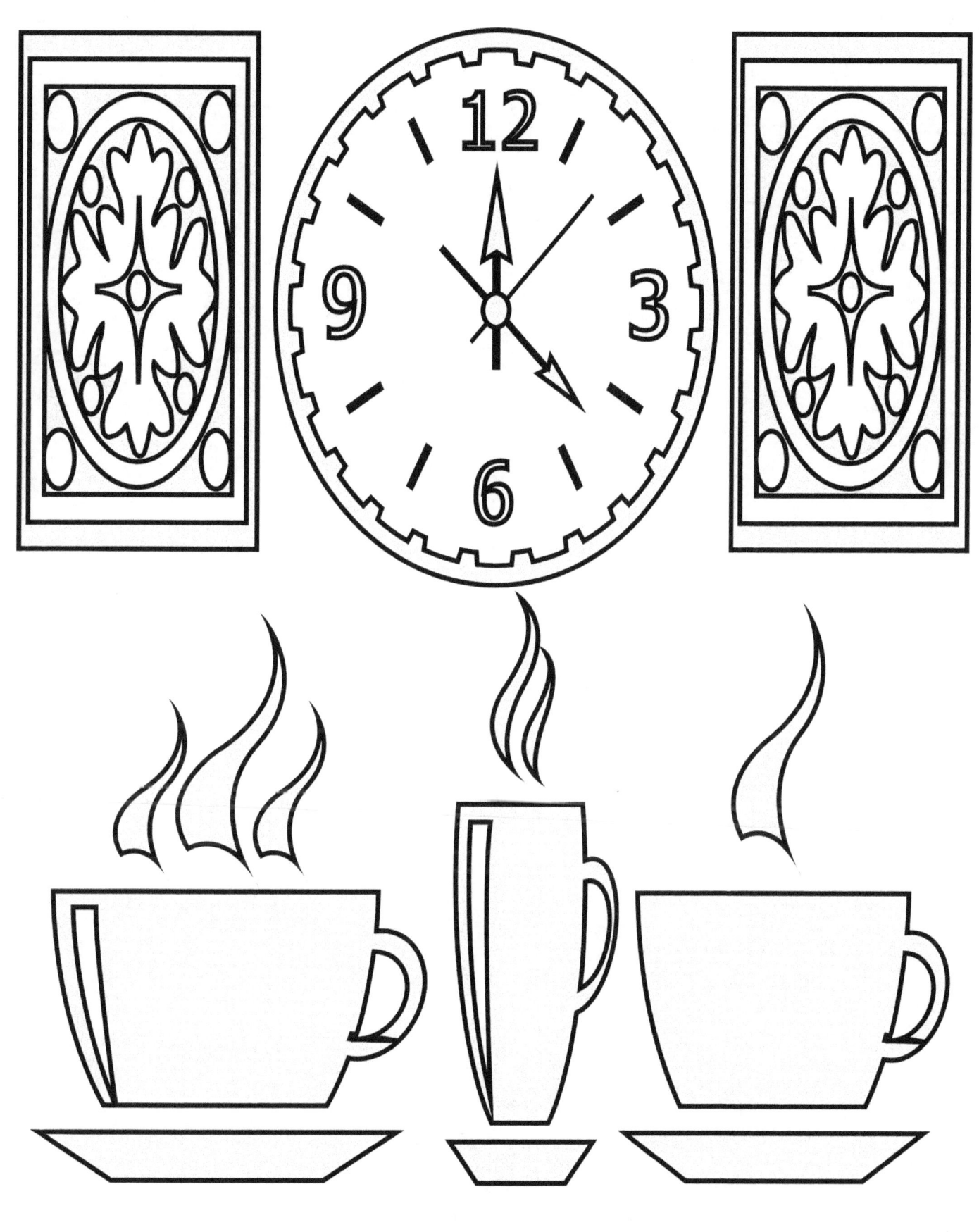

IT'S COFFEE TIME!

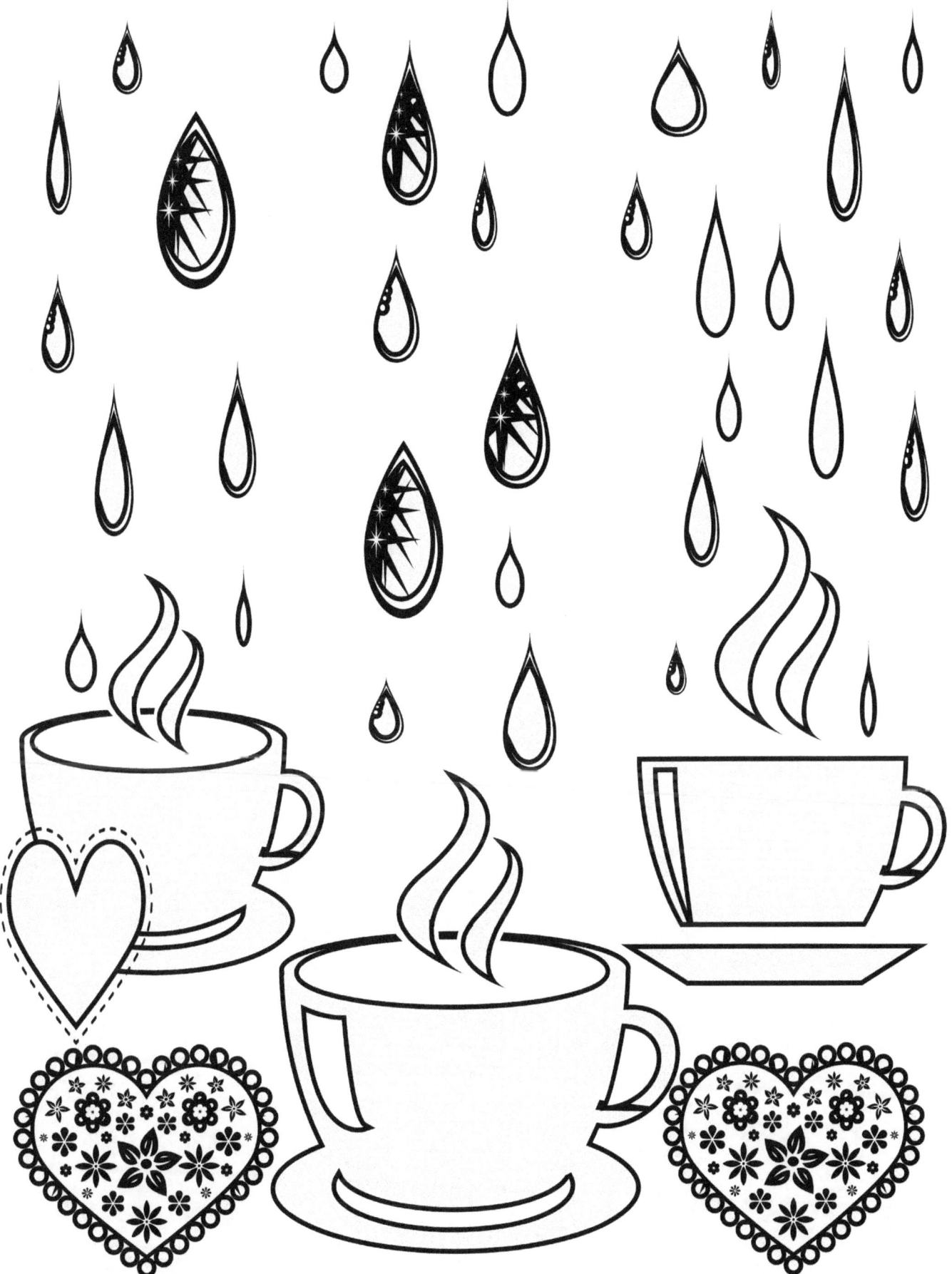

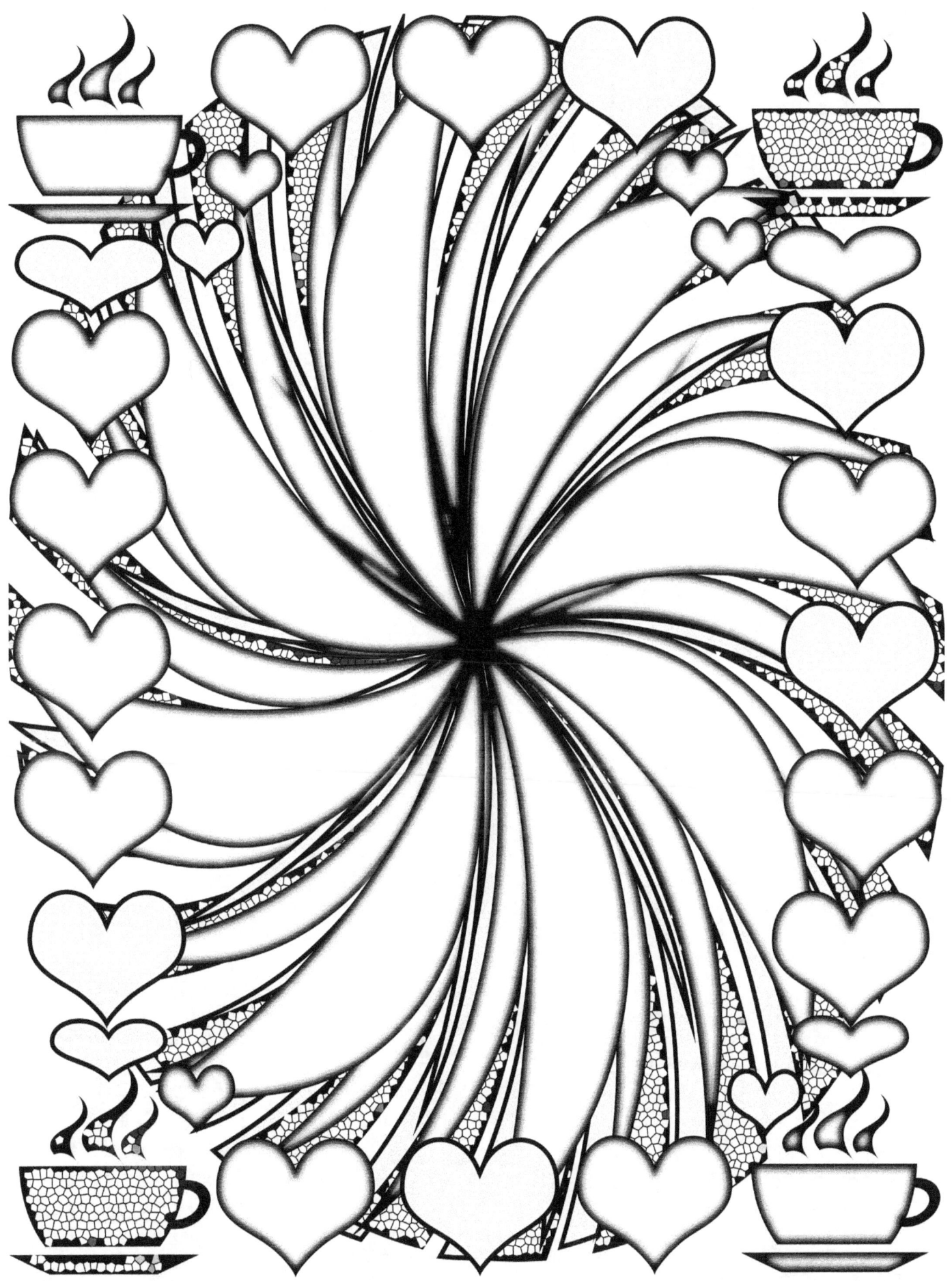

WHAT IS YOUR DRINK OF CHOICE?
COFFEE... TEA... OR...

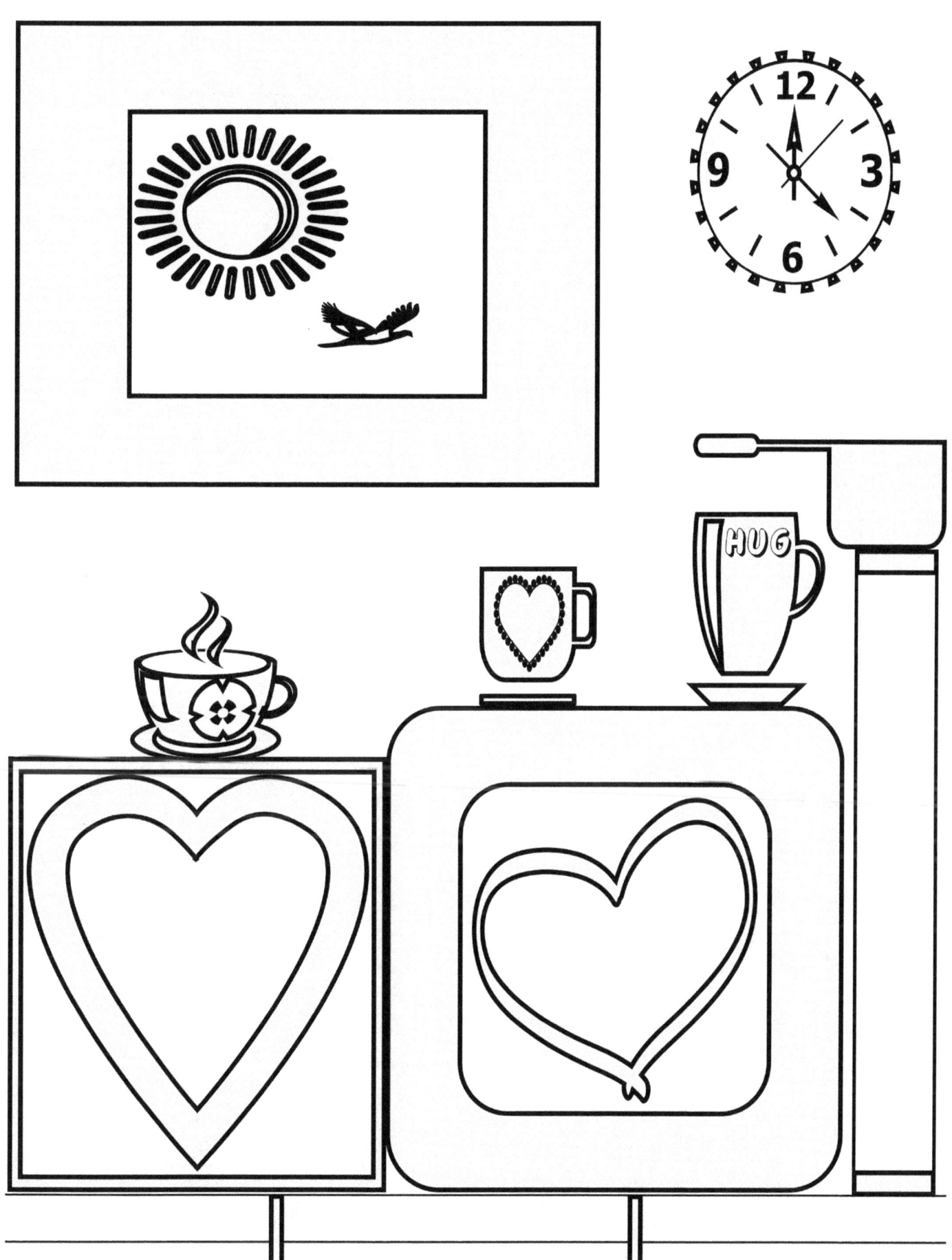

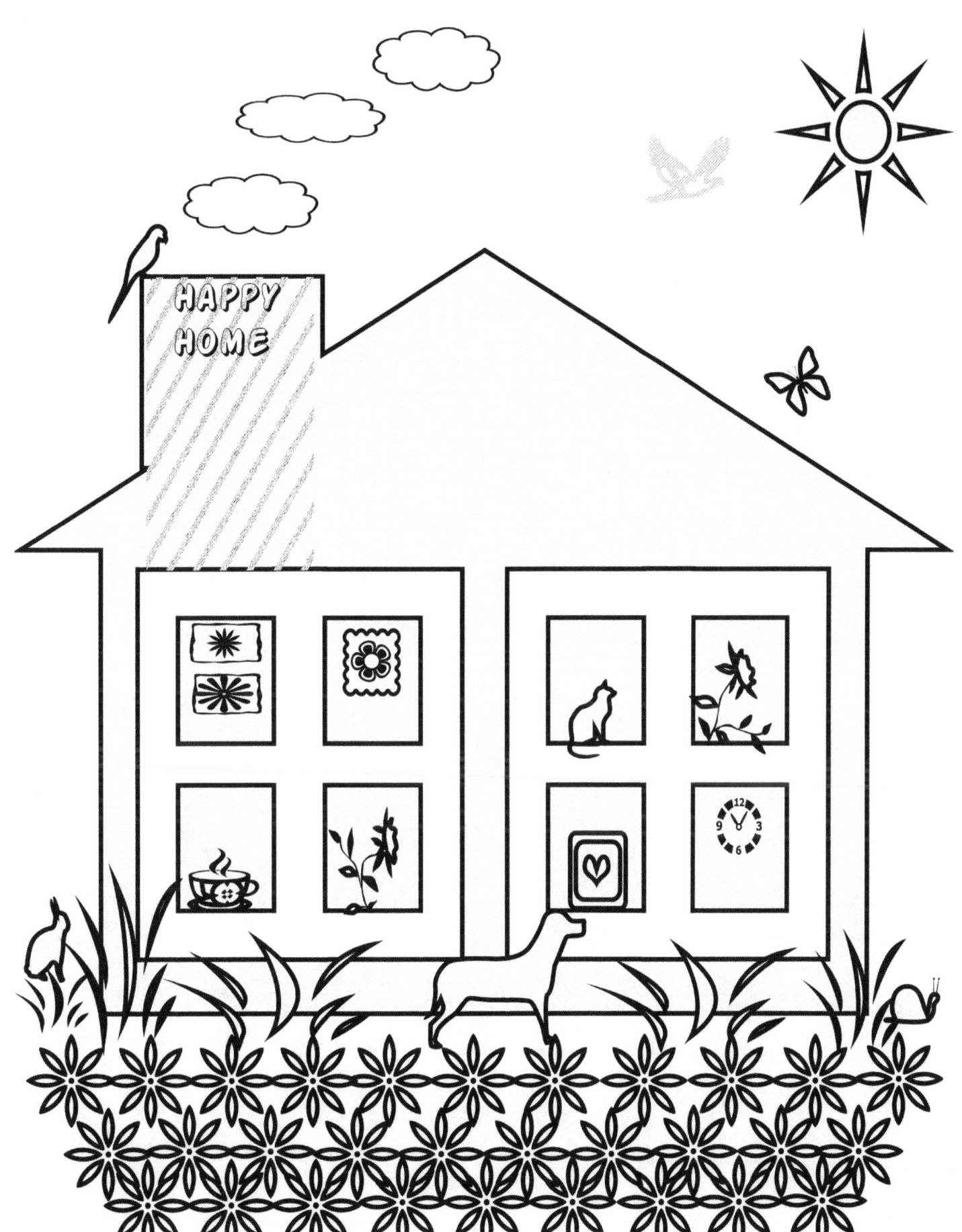

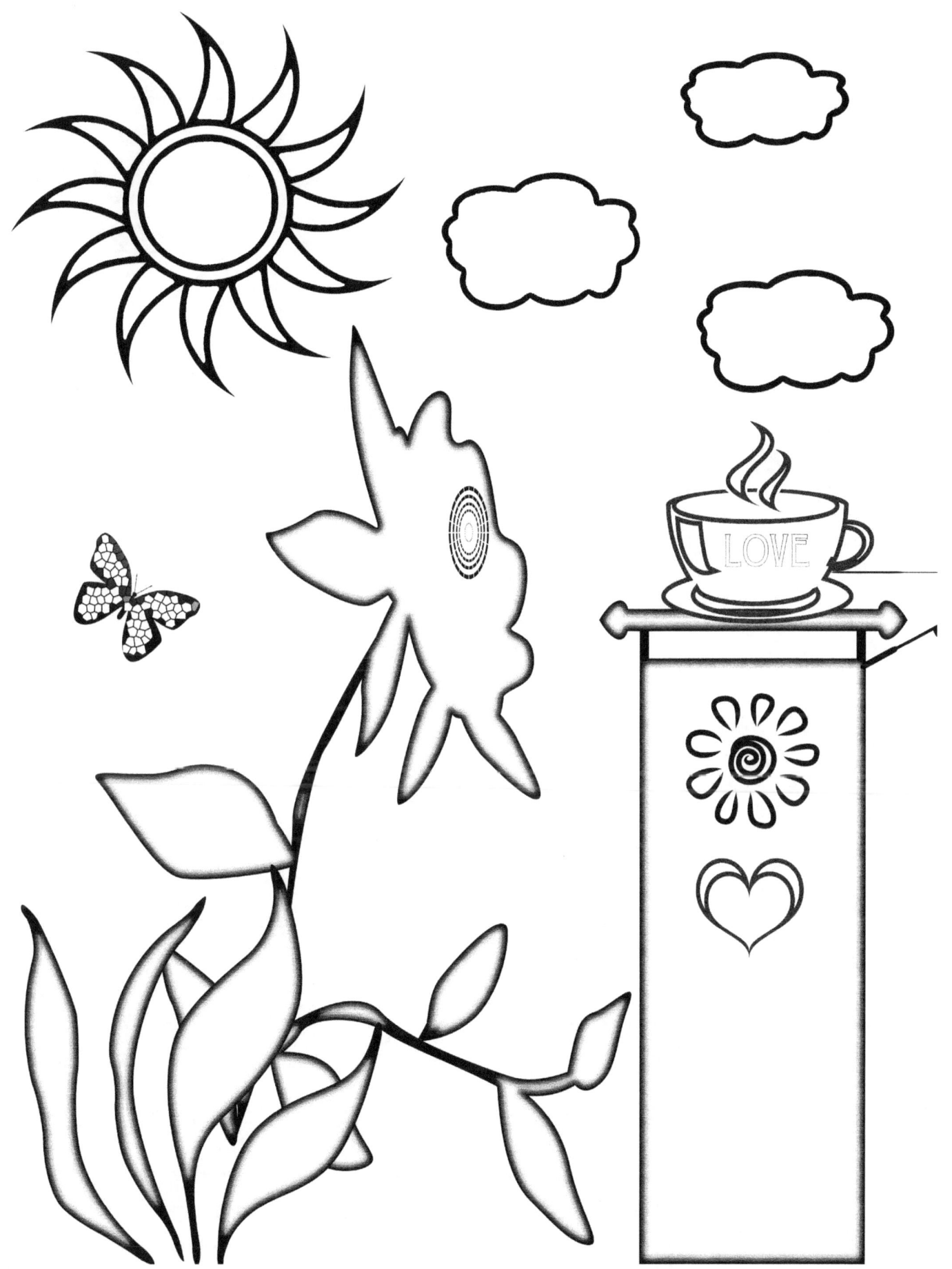

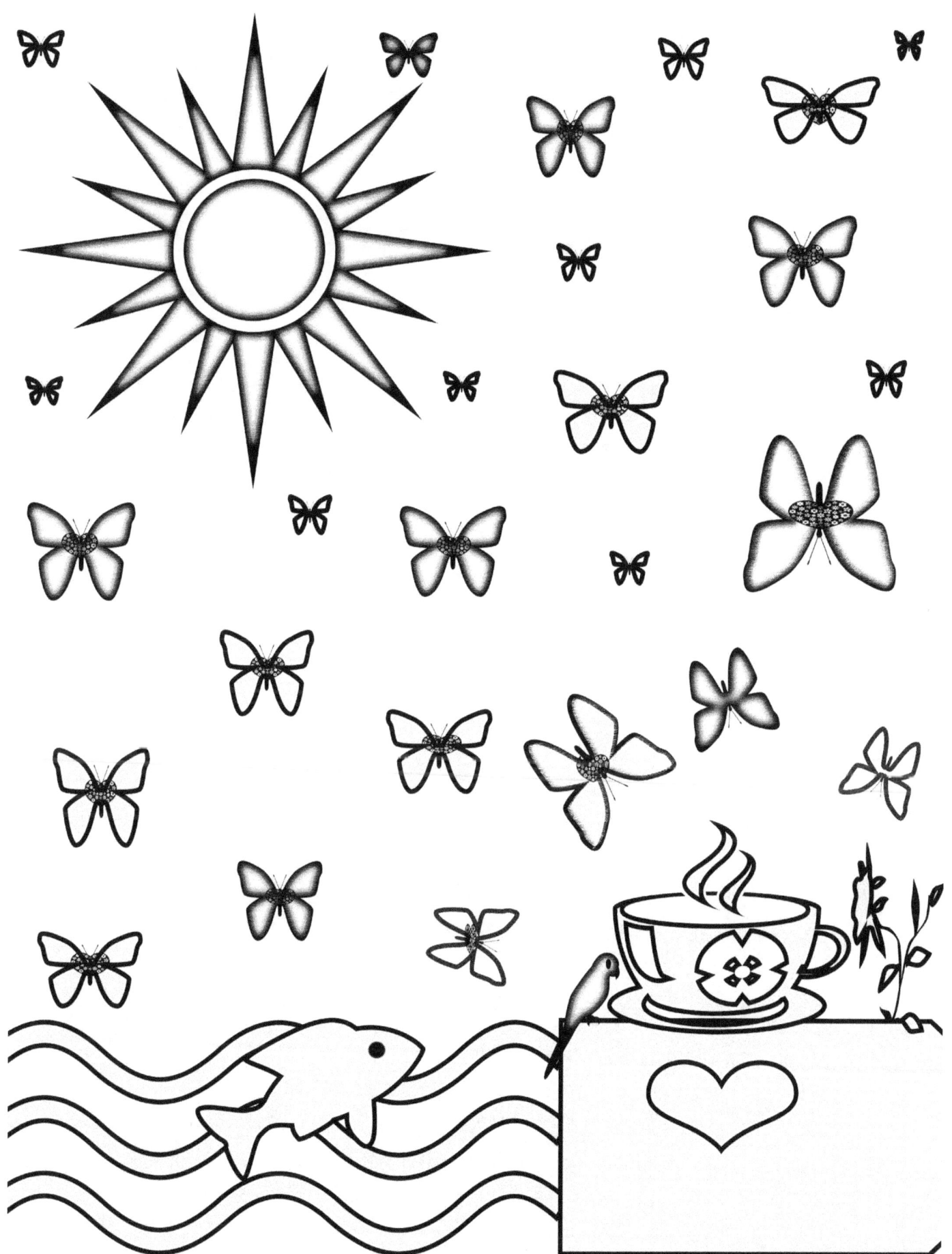

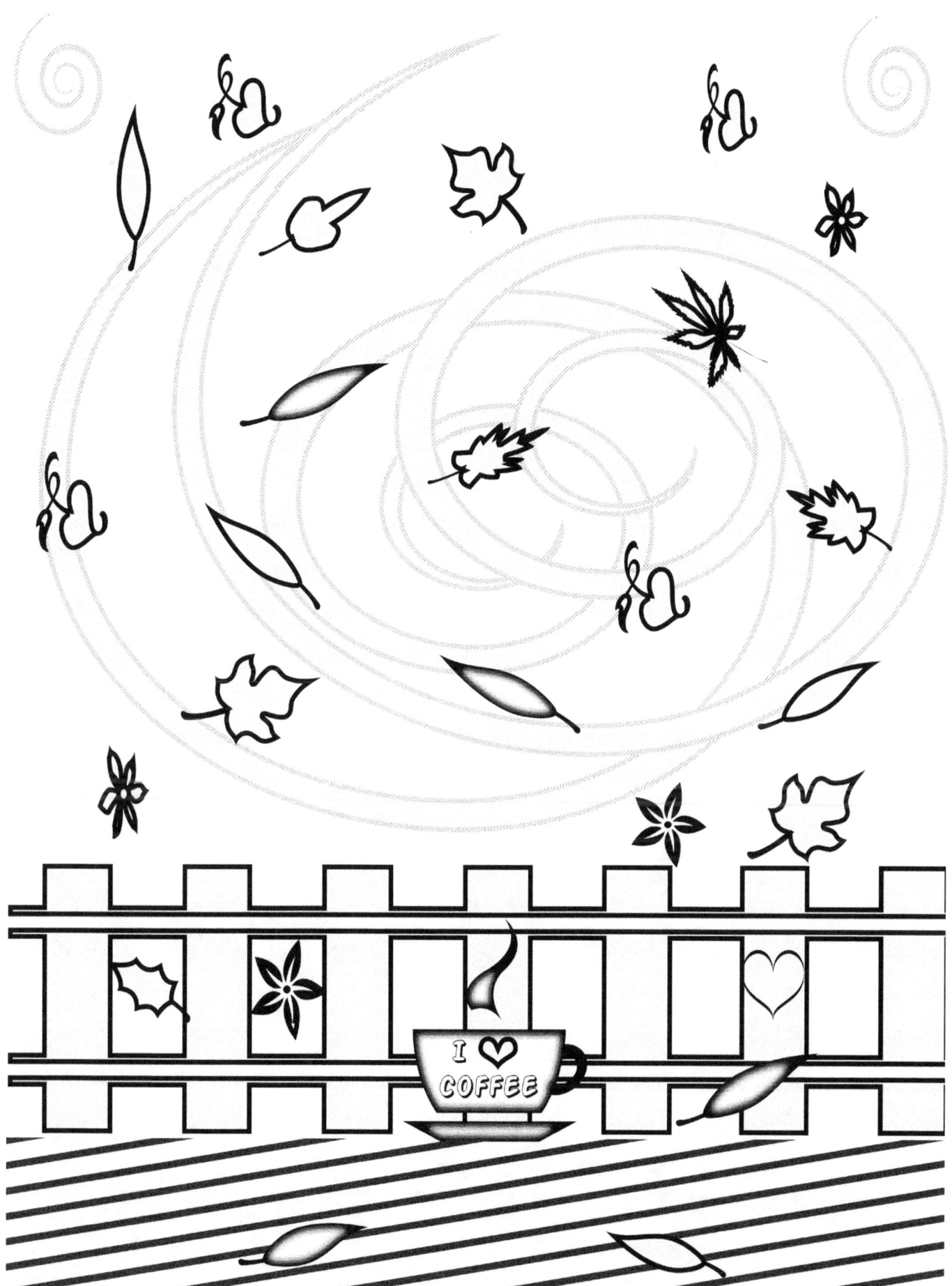

THERE'S
ALWAYS TIME
FOR A FEW MORE
DROPS OF COFFEE
WITH GOOD FRIENDS

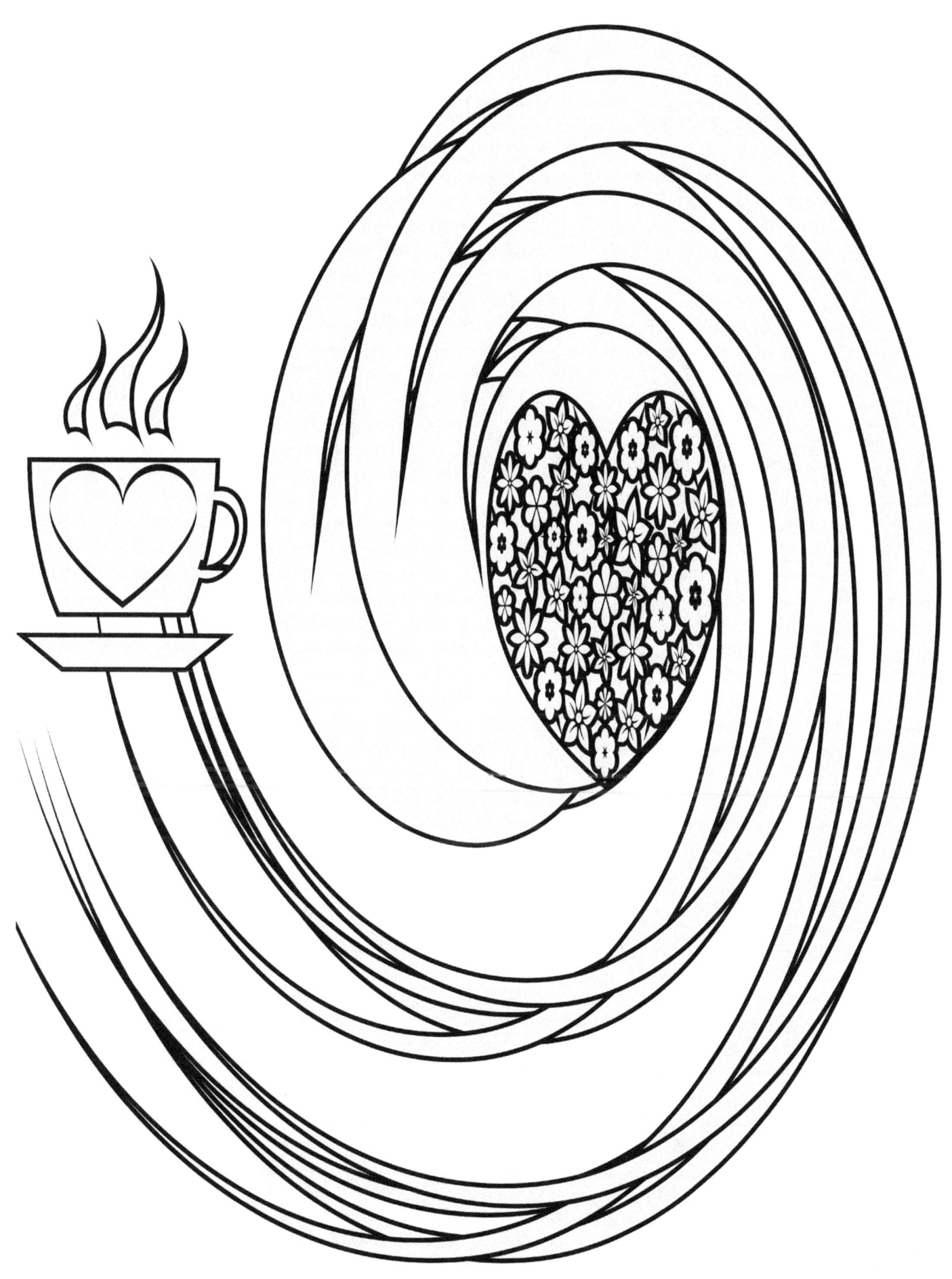

WHAT GOES WITH A PIECE OF CAKE?
COFFEE, COFFEE, COFFEE!

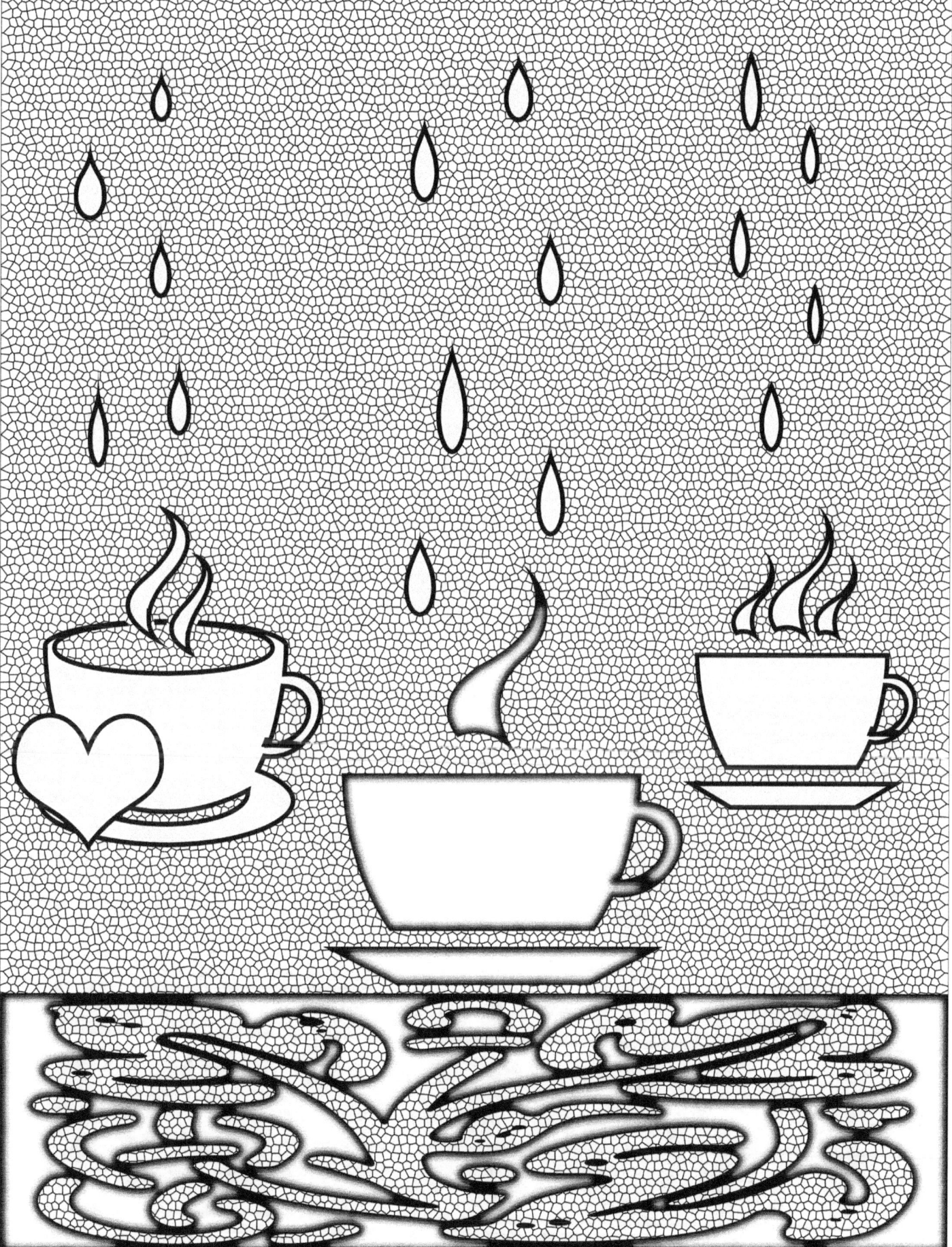

Cheers to my
coffee loving friends!

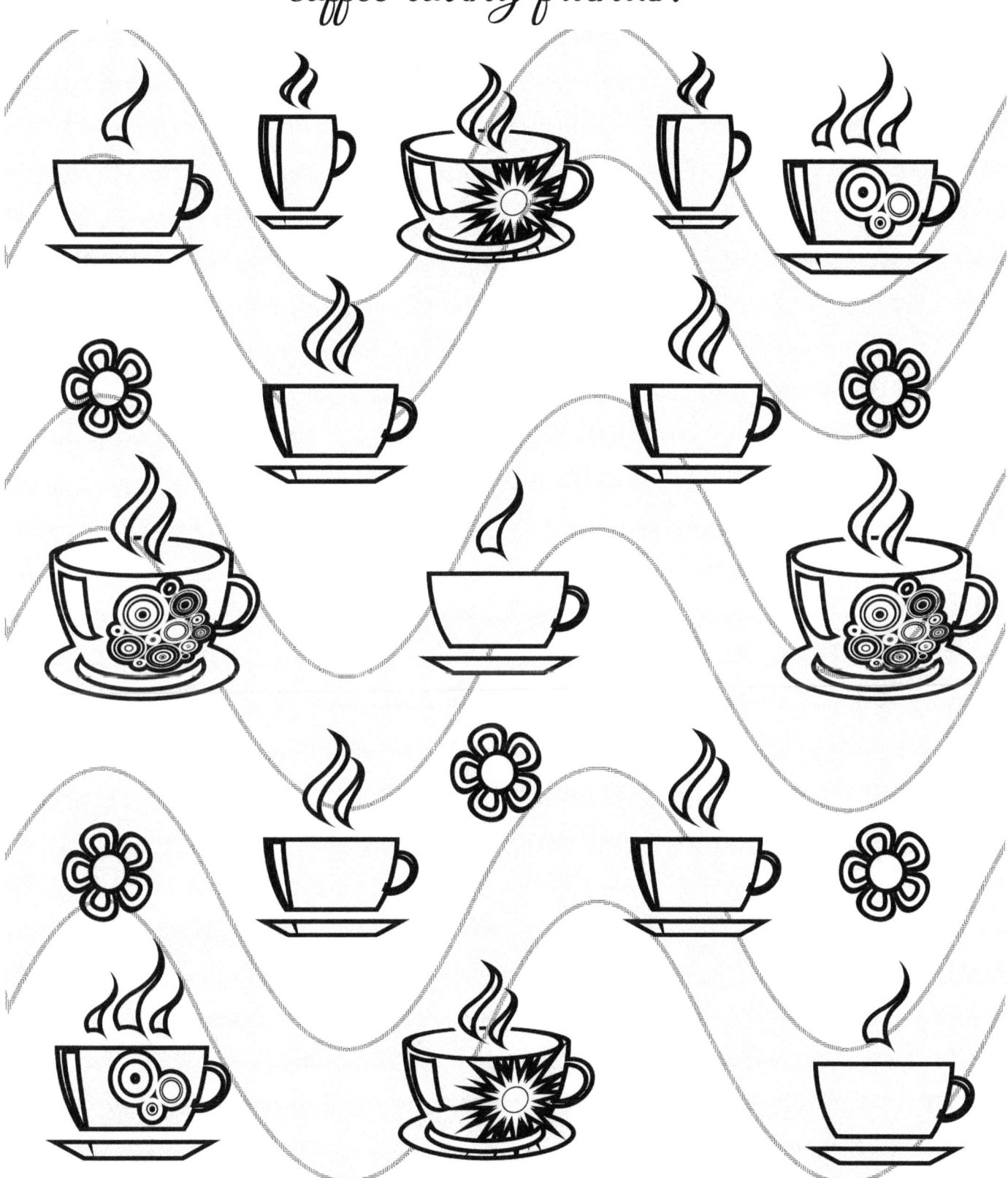